Stranger by Night

Stranger by Night

POEMS

Edward Hirsch

ALFRED A. KNOPF   *New York*   2020

THIS IS A BORZOI BOOK
PUBLISHED BY ALFRED A. KNOPF

www.aaknopf.com

Knopf, Borzoi Books, and the colophon are registered
trademarks of Penguin Random House LLC.

Library of Congress Cataloging-in-Publication Data
Names: Hirsch, Edward, author.
Title: Stranger by night : poems / Edward Hirsch.
Description: First edition. | New York : Alfred A. Knopf, 2020. | "This is
a Borzoi book published by Alfred A. Knopf"
Identifiers: LCCN 2019022482 (print) | LCCN 2019022483 (ebook) | ISBN
9780525657781 (hardcover) | ISBN 9780525657798 (ebook)
Classification: LCC PS3558.I64 A6 2020 (print) | LCC PS3558.I64 (ebook) |
DDC 811/.54—dc23
LC record available at https://lccn.loc.gov/2019022482
LC ebook record available at https://lccn.loc.gov/2019022483

Jacket design by Tyler Comrie

Manufactured in the United States of America

First Edition

Traveler, I am the grave of Biton:
if you go from Torone to Amphipolis,
give Nicagoras this message: his only son
died in a storm, in early winter, before sunrise.

—EPITAPH BY NIKAINETOS, *third century BCE*

CONTENTS

Stranger by Night

My Friends Don't Get Buried

My friends don't get buried
in cemeteries anymore, their wives
can't stand the sadness
of funerals, the spectacle
of wreaths and prayers, tear-soaked
speeches delivered from the altar,
all those lies and encomiums,
the suffocating smell of flowers
filling everything.
No more undertakers in black suits
clutching handkerchiefs,
old buddies weeping in corners,
telling off-color stories, nipping shots,
no more covered mirrors,
black dresses, skullcaps, and crucifixes.
Sometimes it takes me a year or two
to get out to the backyard in Sheffield
or Fresno, those tall ashes scattered
under a tree somewhere in a park
somewhere in New Jersey.
I am a delinquent mourner
stepping on pinecones, forgetting to pray.
But the mourning goes on anyway
because my friends keep dying
without a schedule,
without even a funeral,
while the silence
drums us from the other side,
the suffocating smell of flowers
fills everything, always,
the darkness grows warmer, then colder,
I just have to lie down on the grass
and press my mouth to the earth
to call them
so they would answer.

The Black Dress

I don't know why I opened her book
almost randomly, on a whim,
it signaled me from the shelf
after all these years, like a burning
black dress tangled in the branches,
her dress, she was the one
who was burning,
and that's when the letter fell out,
a love letter, sort of, after we'd given up
on each other, or did we?,
our impossibility,
and suddenly it came back to me
in a rush, that night in Boston,
a restaurant on the harbor, a storm
simmering outside, that slinky
black dress she was wearing,
I didn't know she was burning
inside of it, I thought
it was the coming storm,
summer lightning,
I didn't know I was turning
the pages of her book, her body,
which I would read so closely,
I wanted it so desperately,
she was the fire, I didn't know
she was already mourning
for her childhood in the orchard,
her lost self, forgive me,
I didn't know she was burning
when she took off that black dress.

The Unveiling

Instead of a pebble to mark our grief
or a coin to ease his passage
you placed a speaker
at the top of his head
and suddenly a drumbeat
came blasting out of the grass,
startling the mourners on the far side
of the cemetery, clanging the trees,
scattering the swifts
that had gathered around the stone
like souls of the dead,
souls that were now parting
to make way for a noisy spirit
rising out of the dirt.

The Keening

All morning I heard a thrumming
in the distance, a wail, a wild cry—
atonal, primitive—
so faint and far away
that I tried to blot it out
and follow the news breaking
like a fog over the day,
though I kept hearing it
rising
and coming closer,
a chant,
a plea from the dead
suddenly burning inside me,
one of the grief-stricken ones,
wearing a button-down with a tie
and walking the hall with a notebook
as if I belonged here, as if
I had something else to report.

After the Stroke

(In memory of William Meredith)

Imagine him
standing at the bottom
of an empty well,
raising a broken arm
in darkness
and calling out
to someone, anyone
who may be passing by
but cannot hear
a voice in the ground,
the desperate plea
of a singer whose faith
has not deserted him,
though he is silenced now
like a cello locked
in a black case,
a church bell buried
somewhere in the earth.

The Secret

(*In memory of Richard Rifkind*)

We were watching flamenco dancers
stomping on the stage
and swirling around us,
and I noticed the way he looked at them
with a mixture of curiosity
and contentment, a happiness
free of desire, a state
foreign to me,
and when I asked about it later
he smiled
with such a great sweetness
that it seemed like a light
he had discovered
within himself, a secret
he shared with me once
for a little while,
and I've carried that secret with me
ever since
as a token,
a stone for good luck,
a memory for good fortune.

In Memory of Mark Strand

(Krumville Cemetery, Olivebridge, New York)

I'm not sure why I glanced back
at the bus driver grinding a cigarette butt
with her heel into the gravel driveway.
She was a figure from a myth, from
one of his poems, a stranger, a guardian
marking the passage to the other world.
Maybe she was just another way
of distracting myself from the burial,
from waiting in stunned silence
with the other mourners, all the forlorn
gathered at the graveside without a rabbi
or a priest to lead us in prayer.
It could be said that we were godless,
haunted, lost, as we stood
in the vanishing light and light rain.
Perhaps we had given up too much—
the fundamental beliefs, the consoling rituals—
that would have made the day more bearable.
But as we huddled together in the afternoon,
quivering a little in the chill mist, muffling our sobs,
looking up every now and then at the tall pines,
we felt something lonely moving amongst us,
a current almost, a small gust of wind,
not a ghost exactly, nothing like that,
but the ghost of a feeling, a shiver,
which we might have missed altogether,
except he had changed us, we were changed.

Let's Go Down to the Bayou

Let's go down to the bayou
and cast our sins
into the brown water
on little strips of paper
slowly floating uphill
the way we did that fall
when we moved to Houston
and lived with a small
anonymity
in a large complex
set up for the families
of patients treated
for months
in a nearby hospital
because maybe this time
our neighbor's daughter
with the shaved head
will be healed
and the bayou will accept
our murky sins
the way God never did
and cleanse us.

When You Write the Story

When you write the story
of being a father
don't leave out the joy
of romping up and down
the stairs together
or curving a wiffle ball
across the hallway
or sneaking
past the poor dog
who has fallen asleep
under the grand piano
in the living room
of the house on Sul Ross,
don't forget the giddiness
of eating together
in a secret winter fortress
hidden somewhere—
I'm not saying where—
in someone's backyard,
and what was that song
you invented
to lull him to sleep?
and wasn't it yesterday
that you carried him
down the stairs
to the car humming
in the driveway at five a.m.?

The Radiance

(Detroit, 1984)

Late September
in the shade
outside of State Hall,
that concrete brutality,
where my students are smoking
off a hangover
and gossiping in Ukrainian
while Dan Hughes leans on his walker
and talks to me about Shelley's
bright destructions.
I did not know it was indelible—
the sun spangling the campus trees,
the traffic thickening the smog
outside the museum on Woodward,
our voices rising.
When you tell the story
of those years
going up in flames,
don't forget the radiance
of that day in autumn
burning out of time.

Riding Nowhere

(In memory of Philip Levine)

After all these years
I still can't forget
collecting you
in the snowy darkness
and driving in silence
along Jefferson Avenue
to a local gym
where we stretched
side by side
on stationary bicycles
riding nowhere
at a steady pace
in front of a window
framing the Detroit River
that glided on and on
at its own sweet will
under the skyscrapers
churches and factories
glittering together
in the early-morning light.

Let's Get Off the Bus

Let's get off the bus
in 1979
in front of the empty fairgrounds
on Eight Mile and Woodward
and stop for a few rounds
at the Last Chance Bar.
The moon is tilted
at a rakish angle
and we can toast the unruly
poets of Detroit
and praise our students
who work three jobs
and still show up for class.
Don't get lost
in the sad stories
of the regulars
and make sure to step over
the junkies on the corner
and dodge the cars barreling
past the stoplights
for the suburbs.
Let's surprise my wife
who is napping off her grief
and crank up the stereo
for Stevie Wonder's road trip
through *The Secret Life of Plants*.
Someone has started a garden
on the far side of Palmer Park—
or is it Woodlawn Cemetery?—
where we can throw a party
for our friends
who are still alive.

In the Valley

What was teaching
in that first Pennsylvania winter
but listening to directions
and learning how to drive
on icy two-lane roads
from Easton to Bethlehem?
You were tested
by a deer standing starkly
on the yellow line
and a dead opossum
freezing in the gravel
and the radio playing spirituals
about going home
on a lonesome highway.
The sun skidded to a halt
in the smokestacks
over the river
and I can still see you
climbing the snowy hills
and coasting
past the empty factories
and abandoned warehouses
to a Catholic school
on the edge of town.
You were a skeptic
in the Valley of the Lord
who carried "Pied Beauty"
in your jacket pocket
and drank scalding coffee
in the teacher's lounge
with two old priests
and a lanky young nun
who played pickup basketball
and noticed all things

counter, original, spare, strange.
What was teaching
but quieting a classroom
and learning how to stand
at a blackboard
with an open book
and praise
the unfathomable
mystery of being
to children writing poems
or prayers
in the failing blue light
of a weekday afternoon?

What Is Happiness?

What is happiness anyway?
someone wondered aloud
at the lingering party on the lawn,
and all at once
I was catapulted back
into a raucous second-grade classroom
in northern Pennsylvania,
everyone clamoring with memories
of wading naked
into the Susquehanna River,
running wildly over sandstone
and shales, jumping over
concrete dividers, steel railings,
the whole family pointing together
at the peak of North Knob...
I stood at the blackboard
calling out names
and noting it all down,
marveling
at so much jubilance,
fully absorbed in our creation.

Windber Field

I don't know why
I thought it was a good idea
to bring Wilfred Owen's poem
on the colliery disaster of 1918
to that tiny high school class
in western Pennsylvania,
but soon they were writing
about smokeless coal
and black seams
in the ground, the terror
of firedamp, the Rolling Mill
Mine Disaster in Johnstown,
the closing of Windber Field,
the memory of standing
in a wide ring
around a mine shaft
to watch a man emerge
from the earth
like a god, a father
in an open cage
sailing across the sky.

Night Class in Daisytown

I was failing
my night class
for the eleven parents
of my students
in the Conemaugh Valley
when I mentioned
as if by accident—
or was it desperation?—
the Pitman Poet of Percy Main,
who worked the mines
in Northumberland
and wrote songs and
carols for the coalfields,
and before long
I was standing there
with a piece of fresh chalk
collecting memories
about coal in Cambria County,
the pickaxe and the lantern
hanging by the front door,
the father-in-law
who woke up in the dark
and worked all day in the dark
and slept with a night light,
the mother who whispered
about blackdamp, the brother
who got lost for twenty-four hours
in the underworld
and then found a steel cable
glinting in a mine shaft
and pulled himself
into the light.

The Stony Creek

I drove along the Stony Creek
past the coal piles
and the abandoned mine land
to a little company town
without a company,
a community
where I parked the car
in front of a church
in foreclosure
and crossed the street
to the first school
that would let me teach
all day
until it was time
to drive home again
past the pockmarked land
and the dark caves, the moon
glinting through the gloam
like a headlamp,
heat lightning
in the distance, a storm
sweeping slowly
across the thunderous sky
over the mountains.

In the Endless Mountains

Early morning.
I still remember
the wild cherry tree
behind an empty train station
in the Endless Mountains
of Pennsylvania.
I was traveling to teach
Japanese poetry,
stray flashes of beauty,
to a high school classroom,
but for a moment
I sat down on a wooden bench
flooded with sunlight.
Nothing moved,
time stopped like a question
on the dusty clock in the corner,
and blue swallows
hovered over
the fire cherry.
I could hear an endless hush
in the mountains.

Days of 1975

It started with the tattered blue secret
of Bashō, that windswept spirit,
riding my back pocket for luck.
It started with a walk
through the woods at dawn,
mud on my new shoes,
high humming in the trees.
I was not prepared for the scent
of freshly turned soil
to pervade the empty classroom
or the morning to commence
with a bell that did not stop
ringing in my head.
So many expectations filed
noisily into the room—
I was ready to begin.
From the tall windows
I could see a storefront church
opening on the other side
of the polluted river.
I remember walking past the rows
and rows of bent heads,
scarred desks,
and gazing up
at the Endless Mountains.
In those hopeful days of 1975
I drove the country roads
in honor of radiance.
O spirit of poetry,
souls of those I have loved,
come back to teach me again.

Are You a Narc?

I don't know what possessed you
to step into that small joint
near Penn Station
at rush hour on a Thursday night
in late summer,
but at twenty-four
you should have known
enough to leave
when the room quieted
and everyone swiveled around
to look at you
before turning back to their drinks.
You were too embarrassed
or clueless to turn back
in those days
and so you sat down
at the bar next to a woman
in a postal uniform
who advised you
to make the smart play
and leave forty bucks
on the counter
and head for the door
while you could still walk.

The Iron Gate

Don't look for the Warsaw Ghetto
on a Polish map
in 1974,
it's not there,
don't show up at the Iron Gate
and try to enter
the Second Polish Republic,
there's no guidebook to the trauma
of the Muranów neighborhood,
there's no sign to guide you
through the bloody streets
of the Uprising,
the War
that destroyed the city
where you've come
to see what's been lost,
what's been rebuilt,
though you walk for days
on end without understanding
where you are, where
you've been, the desperation
growing inside of you
when you lie down at night
in a youth hostel
and feel the darkness
pressing through the treetops,
the sound
of something wild
brushing against the window,
a winter fever, a terror
in the wind, the ghosts
of your ancestors
pushing apart the fence
outside the building.

The Fencer

That nightclub on the fringe
of the Old Town
doesn't exist anymore
and neither does that night
when you flirted
with a fencer
who challenged you
to head home with her
for a duel
in the early morning
that somehow lasted
for a few months
in a tiny one-room apartment
in a concrete block
of Soviet housing,
and every day she took you
to watch her thrust and parry
at a gymnasium
where she foiled
her opponents and then
sported with you afterwards
like a young warrior
coming home from battle
to another kind of match
since the two of you never spoke
any language beside the body.

An Unexpected Mirror

(In memory of Zalman Ginsburg)

I strolled down Nevsky Prospekt
on a snowy morning
and dipped into the Kazan Cathedral
for warmth like the Nose
wearing blue jeans and a work shirt
under my father's army coat
in the winter of 1973
when you could still use
foreign currency
in a dollar shop and plot
a basic speech in Russian
(*Meenya zavoot Edward Hirsch…*)
and descended into the metro
carrying a slip of paper
with an address on it
that I showed to every person
on the Horizontal Lift
until someone, anyone, probably
an emissary from the secret police
who was tailing foreigners,
steered me to the #2 line
that ran all the way
to the outskirts of Leningrad,
where I wandered around
an industrial park
until someone else, probably
another agent or informant,
took me by the arm
to a row of twelve-story buildings
on Trade Union Street,
where I climbed
five flights of dimly lit stairs

so I could knock
and knock
on a fortified metal door
that was finally opened
by a man who tilted his head
the way I do
and stood there gazing
into an unexpected mirror
for an eternity
before he recognized
the greenish-brown eyes
and the long knife of his own nose.

Don't Hitchhike

Don't hitchhike
the Mediterranean coast
of Algeria
in the summer of 1971
with only a worn copy
of *The Plague* to guide you
through the dust of Oran,
it won't help
in the city of two lions,
and don't catch a ride
on a six-wheel truck
with a driver
who will make a pass
on a narrow two-lane highway
snaking over the sea,
and avoid sleeping on the beach
outside the port of Annaba,
the site of Aphrodisium,
where you'll be surprised
in the early morning
by six or seven toughs
who circle you on the sand,
one of them has a knife,
and whatever you do
don't hold on to your army bag
when he snatches it away
from you let it go, you're wearing
a money belt anyway,
it's only your notebook of poems,
don't cling to it or you'll get cut
by a switchblade,
but when you do suffer a gash
across a knuckle on your right hand
that won't stop bleeding,

take a bus
to a hospital in Hussein Dey
where a doctor will sew you up—
you have the scar to prove it—
and tell you how Annaba
is plagued by gangsters
like Al Capone
and Baby Face Nelson,
who used machine guns
to shoot up your hometown.

Waste Management

(Skokie, 1970)

Punch the time clock
and try to keep up
with the two collectors
who trained you
since they need to finish
the route in five hours
and get to their second jobs
on time, move steadily
behind the truck,
don't stop to rest
in the shade
between the houses,
don't dawdle or slip
on the gravel
in the alley, watch out
for needles
and broken glass,
it's hot as a dustbowl
in August, but don't wipe
the sweat from your face
with your glove
or your torn sleeve,
lift the trash cans
with your whole body,
don't embarrass yourself
and wave to a girl
from the step
of the garbage truck
racing down Niles Center Road
on the way to the dump
at the end of the day,
don't roll on the carpet

in rage when you get home
or slam the door to your room
and topple the trophies,
never turn yellow-eyed
with hepatitis
and land in the hospital
just to be seen.

On the Engine

You could almost forget
you were coupling
and uncoupling
freight cars
at a hump yard
on the graveyard shift
at Belt Railway
when you rode south
on the engine
slowly looping around
the Chicago Loop
at four a.m.
with only the wind
and the buckling rails
for company
while the city slept
and the lake restlessly
tossed and turned
under a sky
quilted with stars.

The Brakeman

He had a metal plate
welded into the right side
of his head
from a drunken bar fight
that he lost
one night in 1963
outside the Clearing Yard,
where he taught me
how to separate
freight cars
at the top of the hump
and switch them
onto different tracks,
chasing the runaways
and scampering up
the ladder
to set the brakes
and stop the bastards
in their tracks,
parking their bodies
in the rust-colored air
long enough
to recouple, reroute,
and reload them
for shipping
to Iowa or Nebraska
or Colorado, the state
of his retirement,
the wide-open country
where it's possible to see
for hundreds of miles,
and think clearly again,
and breathe
like a free man
in the mountains.

That's the Job

That's the job, he said,
shrugging his shoulders
and running his hand
through his hair, like Dante
or a spider
who knows its web,
that's just the job,
he repeated stubbornly
whenever I complained
about working the night shift
in hundred-degree heat,
or hauling my ass
over the hump
for a foul-mouthed dispatcher
yelling at us
over a loudspeaker,
or riding the cab
of an iron dungeon
creeping over bumpy rails
to a steel mill
rising out of the smog
in Joliet or Calumet City,
where we headed
to track down
a few hundred giants
in chains clanking together
on rusty wheels
for dragging home
and uncoupling
at the Clearing Yard
loaded with empty
freight cars
waiting to be loaded
with more freight
because that's the job.

I Rang the Bell

I rang the bell
to the past
and the owner let me in
so I could climb
seven steps
and stand in the doorway
of a narrowness
that was once my room
on the second floor
of a split-level house
on the corner
of a suburban development
in the village
of my adolescence
and time bent me back
to that fitful night
when I tried to scale
the rusty stairs
of a freight train rolling
out of control in the yard
so I could set the brakes
and stop the runaway
dead in his tracks
but instead
I pulled a bookcase
down on my body
and woke up
startled
to find my parents
frightened in the hallway
and my books—
or was it my future?—
scattered on the floor.

I Missed the Demonstration

I was late getting away
from my shift at the rail yard
and missed the rally
on the steps of the Art Institute
where two college kids
from Normal
burnt their draft cards
and stomped on the flag
in front of the stone lions,
I missed the demonstration
but I could still smell
the tear gas in Grant Park,
where I met a couple
headed off
to join a commune
in northwestern Canada,
and got in an argument
with a pimply faced teenager
from Cicero
who had enlisted
in the Marine Corps
so he could be shipped
to Vietnam or Cambodia,
he didn't care which,
he wanted to fight,
we were all moving
so fast then
it's hard to reconstruct
how history catches us
in its grip
or passes us by,
I missed the demonstration
and brooded about it
on the way home

since there are no accidents,
or so Freud believed,
though I almost corkscrewed
my first car
when a motorcycle
skittered on the gravel
under the overpass
and veered
toward oncoming traffic.

In the Freezer

(Chicago, 1967)

Don't panic
when you step into
the dimly lit freezer
in the basement
of Purity Delicatessen,
where you are lifting
a fifty-pound bag of ice
to carry upstairs
for the umpteenth time
and trying not to fall
through a hole
in the afternoon
where you once got lost
for a moment
in the never-ending cold.

To My Seventeen-Year-Old Self

Your friends are sniffing glue
from a paper bag
in the back of an Impala
tooling around Niles
and Morton Grove
looking for something
to escape
whatever boredom
or childhood damage
everyone suffers,
but don't get high
with them
in a sputtering car
that your girlfriend
refuses to enter,
don't lie to her
after she moves away
and lie down with her friend,
don't sob in the locker room
after the game
or lose your mind
from repeated blows
to the head
on the football field
at Niles West High School,
I mean whatever locker
you hit or don't hit
in desperation
born of the suburbs,
just stand and wait
for the unexpected night
when poetry climbs through
the unlocked window
in the basement

of the split-level house
on Sherwin Avenue
and sits down at your desk.

Chemistry Lesson

(Chicago, 1966)

"There's a simple formula
for getting along here:
don't call me Moon-head,
don't try to fuck
the girls on the floor,
and don't break the beakers
or the Bunsen burners
when you slip them
into boxes. Don't drop
the Petri dishes
or the porcelain crucibles
when you stack them
onto pallets
and don't crash the forklift
when you carry shit
through the aisles
to the loading dock
at the back of the warehouse.
One of the truckers
will take you with him
to unload
on those palaces
of higher education
where a bunch of assholes
wearing lab coats
will botch the experiments
and blame the textbooks,
which we also supply.
If you come back tomorrow
I'll walk you over
to the plant
where we house chemicals,
but try not to breathe."

Someone Is Always Shouting

Moon-head is shouting at me
to back the fuck up
on the forklift
I am trying to jab
into a tower
of wooden pallets
stacked all the way
to the sprinklers
laid out under the roof
of the warehouse
where I am struggling
to control the prongs
of a monster
and avoid dousing
everyone on the floor
of E. H. Sargent & Co.,
my summer in chemicals,
the school where I learned
that someone
is always shouting
at someone else on the job
to back the fuck up.

Snapshot of My Natural Father

I wish I could find
the snapshot of him standing
in front of the Flamingo Hotel
in Las Vegas, the dream child
of Bugsy Siegel and Meyer Lansky,
his two favorite gangsters,
the killers who created the strip
of garishness and greed
in the desert, that mecca
which loomed as a short flight
from Phoenix, he could go
on a dare or a hunch
for a twenty-four-hour play
and then stroll back
into the office Monday morning
ready to take advantage
of anyone who walked through
the door to sell scrap metal,
he came by it honestly,
he said, his need to deal
and get the upper hand,
he didn't care how he won,
I couldn't tell if he was bluffing
when we crowded around
the poker table for his birthday
and he boasted
that he always wanted to join
the Bugs and Meyer Mob,
Murder, Inc.,
but he was too young
and didn't have one thing
it takes to succeed,
physical courage.

The Elevated Train

Yesterday I climbed the stairs
and took the "L"
to 1965
where I was stuck
in the heart
of downtown Chicago
waiting for my grandmother
to finish her shift
in the coat department
at Three Sisters
so she could treat me
to a luxurious dinner
at Fritzel's
before she disappeared
into the elevated train
that carried her
to a station
near her studio apartment
in a third-floor walk-up
on Lawrence Avenue
where she turned on the TV
for company
to drown out the noise
rattling
from the tracks.

A Small Tribe

The legend
of a small tribe
who crossed the steppes
to become Eastern European
eyeglass grinders
with weak eyesight,
horse traders, deserters
from the Russian army,
peddlers, impractical merchants,
men who cried
at the sad stories of women
in tenements, who made
their mothers laugh
over steaming cups of coffee
at the kitchen table,
social democrats
who argued with anarchists
and communists, Zionists
who never travelled to Zion,
failed businessmen
who snuck into Carnegie Hall
to hear Rubinstein playing Chopin
and then stood on a soapbox
in Union Square shouting for justice
in the Spanish Civil War,
who loved used-book stores
and the musty back stacks
of old libraries
but started a drugstore in Rochester
or sat on his suitcase
waiting for the train
to misfortune
selling shirts on Maxwell Street,
asthmatics, non-assimilators

whose daughters
married developers
who never developed
and scrap-metal dealers
looking for an honest advantage,
a gambler who beat the house
and lost everything
three times, a box salesman
who could not contain himself,
a scribbler, my favorite
was a daydreamer
who bought a new hat
every year for Passover
so that he could stand outside
the temple,
which he refused to enter,
though he loved the songs
and wanted to be close
to the prayers.

The Guild

Goodbye to the years
we spent leaning
over badly typed poems
in cramped studies
and dank hotel rooms,
half-crazed, inconsolable,
constantly jabbing pencils
at each other, brooding,
smoking on the balcony
across from a temple
on the other side of the river
one night in Rome, loyal
or disloyal to the old gods,
our flawed mentors,
our weakness for standing
at the podium
seeking applause,
slashing lines, reciting Blake
or Yeats, giving up sleep
for late-night sessions
listening to Coltrane
and gossiping
about new books and poets
who have been dead
for centuries,
facing each other
knee to knee
or sitting side by side
over each fresh draft,
furiously arguing
about this enjambment
or that allusion, mysteries
of the craft, the muse,
our shoulders touching,

our voices growing hoarse
with laughter or walking out
to the pier
a few yards from the sea
so that we could stand there
together under the stars,
alone with the abyss.

The Task

You never expected
to spend so many hours
staring down an empty sheet
of lined paper
in the harsh inner light
of an all-night diner,
ruining your heart
over mug after mug
of bitter coffee
and reading Meister Eckhart
or St. John of the Cross
or some other mystic
of nothingness
in a brightly colored booth
next to a window
looking out
at a deserted off-ramp
or unfinished bridge
or garishly lit parking lot
backing up
on Detroit or Houston
or some other city
forsaken at three a.m.
with loners
and insomniacs
facing the darkness
of an interminable night
that stretched into months
and years.

A House of Good Stone

I was like a prosecutor
still presenting evidence
and pressing his case
after the trial
in a house of good stone
cut smooth and well fitting
high on a cliff lodged
over the Pacific
where a group of poets
gathered
and tried to ignore
my indictment
of the murderous voice
on Italian radio ranting
about bankers
and lending rates
and the Chosen People
finagling on the Rialto
in seventeenth-century Venice,
though I wonder now
why I was so invested
in arguing
with my exemplars
who couldn't care less
about Social Credit or usury
or all that nasty blather
about Jews,
but loved *Cathay*,
the way I did,
and carried the *Cantos*
through Italy
like a Virgilian guide,
or visited the Oracle
at St. Elizabeths

and sailed to Greece
with a devotion
to luminous moments,
like the one I recall now,
standing at the window
in a stone house
touched by sunlight
and overlooking the sea.

Every Poem Was a Secret

Every poem was a secret
struggle with himself,
every secret was a struggle,
a handwritten scrawl,
something joyous
or terrible,
a fragmentary
blood-soaked message
wrenched out of his body,
a longing for
some impossible harmony
tucked into a bottle
and tossed off the side of a cliff.
Reckless love poems, shocked elegies
drafted against death
looking for God—
some of them shattered
in desperation
on the rocks below,
but others, like this one,
bobbed away
on surging blue waves
for someone to find them.

I Was an Illiterate Herdsman

I was an illiterate herdsman
abandoned by my god
when I moved
away from the country—
or maybe I had abandoned
my muse
lost in grief
for more than a year
when I was parted
from my flock,
but then a voice
came to me like a dream
and said,
Don't forget
the black-throated
blue warbler
hiding
in the woods,
wake up and sing!

The Window Washer

As if by magic
he dropped out of the sky
on a steel scaffold
and abruptly appeared
perched outside my window
on the 33rd floor.
I glanced up from my desk
a little startled to find
somebody
high up in the air
swiveling a squeegee
on the other side
of the streaked glass.
I waved to him
and then he waved back
before he was lowered down
to another floor
of our interminable skyscraper.
It was a long day working alone
and I felt oddly gleeful
when I saw him later
coming off the job safely
in street clothes, walking on ground.
We nodded as we passed
and when I looked up
I could see the moon balancing
on a rooftop in the distance.

Stranger by Night

After I lost
my peripheral vision
I started getting sideswiped
by pedestrians cutting
in front of me
almost randomly
like memories
I couldn't see coming
as I left the building
at twilight
or stepped gingerly
off the curb
or even just crossed
the wet pavement
to the stairs descending
precipitously
into the subway station
and I apologized
to every one
of those strangers
jostling me
in a world that had grown
stranger by night.

Sometimes I Stumble

No one ever leaves
the building across the street
and I can't explain why
I spent the summer
staring at its blank windows
and stony façade, its caged trees,
while the sun crawled
across the light blue emptiness
yawning with clouds.
I was stunned by grief
into silence, inner muteness.
But then one afternoon
I decided to give up
my watch.
Sometimes I stumble
in shadows, sometimes I trip
over the last stair of the house,
but now when I stroll
toward a prospect
my spirit lifts
with the stirring of nightjars,
the first whip-poor-will of evening.

A Baker Swept By

You were already
losing your eyesight
last winter in Rome
when you paused in the doorway
at nine o'clock on a Saturday morning
and a baker swept by
on a shiny bicycle
waving a cap and singing
under his breath,
you didn't know bakers wore
white aprons dusted with flour
and floated around the city
like angels
on a freshly baked day,
you weren't sure why
morning halted
up and down the street
as you stood in the doorway
and a baker winged by
on a weekend morning
so new and pristine
that you looked into the sky
and for one undiminished instant
of misplaced time
you saw brightness,
brightness everywhere,
before a shadow crossed
the rooftops
and it was blotted out.

I Walked Out of the Cemetery

I put down my prayer book
and sifted through a wave
of fresh mourners
gathering at a nearby grave.
I didn't stop to ask
who had died, I didn't wait
for the eight pallbearers
lurching toward us
with a casket in their hands,
I didn't even pause to wonder
about a young woman
lifting her veil
and applying lipstick
under a long-limbed sycamore
by the side of the road.
For once, I didn't look back.
The dying goes on, it never stops,
there was a new procession
of black sedans
winding down the lane,
but I didn't hesitate
to step around them
on my mission to leave
these hallowed grounds.
I felt so liberated
I couldn't help waving
to a group of teenagers
listening to rowdy music
and drinking beer in the parking lot
behind the chapel.

Don't Write Elegies

Don't write elegies
anymore, let someone else
stumble past the mausoleum
and grieve
under the calm shade
of a plane tree, wiping away
the tears of his ex-wife,
staining the knees of his black suit,
first sobbing, then choking back sobs,
comforting others, consoling himself
by scrubbing the white stone
and weeding the plot
year after year,
I'm sorry, it's too sad, it's time
for someone else to mourn
my dead,
though who else can do it?,
I just need to lie here
a while longer
face down in the soil
and then get up and breathe.

ACKNOWLEDGMENTS

My deep gratitude to Laurie Watel, my shrewdest reader, for figuring out the order of this book, my life.

Special thanks to the editors of the following publications where these poems, some of which have been revised, first appeared:

The American Poetry Review: "Epitaph by Nikainetos, Third Century BCE," "The Keening," "In the Valley," "What Is Happiness?," "Windber Field," "Night Class in Daisytown," "The Stony Creek," "In the Endless Mountains," "Days of 1975"
The Atlantic: "The Unveiling"
The Believer: "Don't Write Elegies"
Bellevue Literary Review: "After the Stroke"
Copper Nickel: "An Unexpected Mirror," "The Black Dress"
Five Points: "The Fencer," "The Elevated Train," "Chemistry Lesson," "Waste Management"
Green Mountains Review: "Let's Go Down to the Bayou," "The Brakeman," "The Window Washer"
Harvard Review: "In Memory of Mark Strand"
The Kenyon Review: "That's the Job," "Someone Is Always Shouting," "The Task"
Literary Imagination: "A Small Tribe," "The Guild," "A House of Good Stone," "Every Poem Was a Secret," "I Was an Illiterate Herdsman"
The Massachusetts Review: "I Rang the Bell"

Michigan Quarterly Review: "The Radiance," "Riding Nowhere," "Let's
   Get Off the Bus"

Narrative: "When You Write the Story," "Don't Hitchhike," "I Missed the
   Demonstration," "To My Seventeen-Year-Old Self," "Snapshot of My
   Natural Father"

The National: "On the Engine"

The New Yorker: "My Friends Don't Get Buried," "A Baker Swept By"

The New York Review of Books: "I Walked Out of the Cemetery"

The Paris Review: "Sometimes I Stumble"

Poetry Athens: "The Iron Gate"

The Threepenny Review: "Stranger by Night"

"Let's Get Off the Bus" also appeared in *Respect: The Poetry of Detroit
   Music* (Michigan State University Press, 2019).

"That's the Job" was reprinted in *Pushcart XLIV* (Pushcart Press, 2018).

"Stranger by Night" was reprinted in *Poetry Daily* and *The Best American
   Poetry 2018* (Scribner, 2019).

Edward Hirsch, a MacArthur Fellow, has published nine previous books of poetry, including *The Living Fire: New and Selected Poems* and *Gabriel: A Poem,* a book-length elegy for his son. He has also published five books of prose, among them *How to Read a Poem and Fall in Love with Poetry,* a national best seller. He has received numerous prizes, including the National Book Critics Circle Award. A longtime teacher, at Wayne State University and in the Creative Writing Program at the University of Houston, Hirsch is now president of the John Simon Guggenheim Memorial Foundation. He lives in Brooklyn.

A NOTE ABOUT THE TYPE

This book was set in Fairfield, a typeface designed by the
distinguished American artist and engraver Rudolph Ruzicka
(1883–1978).

Composed by North Market Street Graphics,
Lancaster, Pennsylvania

Printed and bound by LSC Communications,
Crawfordsville, Indiana

Designed by Michael Collica